The Basic Retirement Planning Guide For 50+

A Simplified Beginners Guide To Retirement Success

Marilyn S. Hiland, Ph.D

Marilyn S. Hiland

Copyright©2022 Marilyn S. Hiland
All Rights Reserved.

THE BASIC RETEIRMENT PLANNING GUIDE FOR 50+

Table of Contents

INTRODUCTION	**4**
CHAPTER 1	**6**
Your retirement begins right now!!!	6
What Exactly People Say About Retirement	13
CHAPTER 2	**22**
When is the right time to retire?	22
Why A Financial Advisor?	26
Diversity Is Key in Retirement Planning	29
CHAPTER 3	**33**
Making financial plans for retirement	33
Individual retirement account (IRA)	36
401(K) plans	42
Health Savings Account (HSA)	46
CHAPTER 4	**50**
Housing, Medicare, and Social Security	50
Housing Issues: An Overview	50
Options for Retirement Housing and Relocation Issues	52
Innovative Housing Choices	54
Medicare Options	56
Social Security's retirement program	61

CHAPTER 5 — 64

How to Invest and Where to Invest — 64
    What Investment Options Do You Have? — 64

Investing in and Profiting From Real Estate — 71
    Real estate investing' drawbacks — 73

CHAPTER 6 — 75

Staying Active in Retirement — 75
    EAT HEALTHY FOODS TO HELP YOU LIVE A HEALTHY LIFE. — 77
    EXERCISE CAN HELP YOU REMAIN HEALTHY. — 78
    STAY HEALTHY BY KEEPING A POSITIVE ATTITUDE. — 80

What to Do in Retirement: 20 Big Ideas — 81

CHAPTER 7 — 97

CONCLUSION — 97

Marilyn S. Hiland

Introduction

It isn't something that the birds do. It's also not something that animals do. However, because we are the only species conscious of its own mortality, we have developed and implemented a retirement phase.

We're told that retirement is inevitable. When you leave your desk or counter and retire to your house, you will live off your retirement funds or Social Security (if it is still available).

Will it, on the other hand, happen to you? And what plans do you have in place to deal with this transition?

In response to the first question, yes, retirement will come to you someday, just as it does to most people between the ages of 60 and 67. You'll wake up one day and not go to work. However, that doesn't imply you'll stop generating income; many seniors continue to work in some way well into their seventies and beyond.

It also doesn't imply that you'll go from working in an office to moving into a nursing home. However, you should expect to be active for at least twenty years, much of it at the same speed and intensity as earlier in life.

As your retirement progresses, you could become more reflective, passionate, grateful, and curious. Alternatively, you may become more lonely, bored, and perhaps broke. This brings us to our next question. What can you do to get ready for your golden years?

As a result, this book emphasizes the need of starting your retirement planning now, before you leave your job. Money, health, friends and family, and engaging activities, in my opinion, are the only things required to retire peacefully. It will be tough to make new friends, reconcile family rifts, and start new activities once you reach the age of 65, just as it would be difficult to save money.

So, how long are you going to wait? You have an undiscovered goldmine in your palm, which will aid you in navigating the curves of the mountainous path ahead of you. Assuring that you have a great time at all times.

Get started with the first chapter. Prepare for your retirement now. It's never too early to start thinking about your future and your ideal retirement.

☐

CHAPTER 1

Your retirement begins right now!!!

Imagine never seeing your mother's smile as a kid. Consider being unable to attend class because the words in your textbooks appear to spill across the pages like ink. Imagine the feeling of helplessness if your livelihood was threatened by a thick fog that obscured your view.

Imagine all of that suffering, heartache, and danger being magically alleviated by the compassionate hands of a foreign doctor who came to your community with a team of volunteers who are willing to treat you for nothing in exchange for the satisfaction of seeing you cured.

Finally, envision yourself as that doctor or volunteer. Because this may be your retirement, or at least a portion of it: making a difference in other people's lives. It has the potential to become a part of the lives of anybody who wants to live a better, more meaningful existence.

This is how Dr Robert Dyson, the real-life doctor referenced above, spends his retirement. He works as a volunteer with Orbis International, a nonprofit organization devoted to preventing preventable blindness worldwide.

After more than 30 years of service at the university and in private practice, Robert, a Professor Emeritus of Ophthalmology and Visual Sciences at the University of Wisconsin, volunteered with Orbis' Flying Eye Hospital and serves as a mentor to aspiring eye health experts in other countries.

Robert has made it a point to give back in his second Act. And it's something that helps both him and the cause he's fighting for. According to research, volunteering has been shown to improve people's emotional and physical well-being, particularly older folks.

So, as you race to put money aside for retirement, remember that money isn't the most crucial aspect of a happy retirement. Instead, concentrate on the things that money can't always buy: a feeling of purpose, contentment, and meaningful connections.

Robert serves as an example of living a happy, purposeful retirement when you dedicate yourself to giving back. I had the opportunity to conduct an email interview with him. He gladly agreed to tell me about his experiences and ideas.

Based on our conversation, here are three life-changing insights from this gentleman who has chosen to devote his later years a time for helping others.

Lesson No. 1: *Your 'calling' doesn't end at retirement.*

In retirement, who will you be?

Yes, retirement allows you to be anyone you choose. However, many people experience a loss when their careers close. More than a quarter (27%) of retirees asked in retirement research indicated they "struggled with the transition from employment to retirement." It's a condition known as "identity distress," and it's prevalent among individuals who have been forced to retire. It's why some individuals are hesitant to retire, fearful of losing their identity and having to remake themselves.

In retirement, it's crucial to maintain one's identity. "Having a purpose is essential to a good retirement," stated nearly all (92 percent) retirees in the Edward Jones/Age Wave research. Finding a sense of purpose does not have to entail a whole makeover. Robert told us in our interview that giving back has allowed him to continue doing the work he loves in a new way.

Robert: *I enjoyed every aspect of my work, including clinical work, surgery, research, and teaching. I believe I enjoyed teaching the most. The only part of my career that I can perform in retirement is teaching. I've had some amazing instructors and mentors, and I know how much of a difference I can make through teaching.*
For retirees who wish to continue participating in their industries, the nonprofit sector has a lot of options. To advance their objectives, many organizations respect the talents and expertise of older persons.

Lesson No. 2: *You can never be too old or experienced to learn something new.*

It's exhausting to be an expert. But, being a learner and letting go of your ego is like sitting at the best banquet you'll ever attend.
Robert has become a student again after travelling to several places and meeting individuals from all backgrounds. It has been a source of enormous personal growth for him, he claims.

Robert: *My head was programmed on my first volunteer trip that I was this wonderful American doctor who would go educate these men a thing or two. When I arrived on the plane, I recognized what excellent doctors my trainees were, how committed they were, and how eager they were to learn. Which made me realize I could still learn a few things from them. Learning about different cultures and individuals is a great experience that I would not have had otherwise.*
In Ghana, I met a woman whose daughter had her sight returned following surgery. The mom was so moved by the fact that her daughter could see clearly again that she offered me her family's cow. I was moved by her story because I understood how important the cow was to her family. It was humbling to learn that she wished to offer it to me as a token of her thanks.

Interactions with people from diverse cultures often need one of the most popular activities: travel. Travel has promoted empathy by exposing people to different people and cultures. So, go off on your journey. Because stagnation is never conducive to progress.

Lesson No. 3: *Variety is the spice of life – and perhaps a happy retirement.*

Retirees frequently enjoy a rush of pleasure and life satisfaction just after they retire, only to see their satisfaction decline a few years later.

What's up with that?

Although retirees are often happier than those who are still working, some people may find retirement unattractive — or even boring — if they have nothing to look forward to or no interests to keep them occupied.
Robert finds meaning in giving back, but he also acknowledges the need of finding joy in other areas, particularly spending time with loved ones.

Robert: *Because I've spent so much of my time concentrating on ophthalmology, I've run out of interest. But I'm thankful that my grandchildren live nearby so that I can spend more time with them. ... I've become friends with a group of people who play* *a lot of golf. I walk around 72 holes every week, which has helped me lose weight and taught me patience. I'm glad medicine was simpler to learn than golf! ... Cooking is something I like doing. Every Thursday, I spend time trying out new dishes and organizing our family photos to piece together my family history.*

According to research published in Nature Neuroscience, exploring new locations and doing new things is excellent for brain growth and pleasure.

As a result, given that your retirement might last decades, it's wise to start exploring new hobbies now, so you don't become bored. The objective is to discover activities that you enjoy so you never run out of things to do.

What Exactly People Say About Retirement

According to a study, many people have different perspectives on retirement. However, just a few stood out.
There are three sorts of retirees. I'll give you an example by telling you about the first one.

I chatted with my father over Sunday dinner three months after he retired and asked if he wanted to come by my office and have lunch with me the following week. "I'll look into it," he said, "but I'll let you know early next week if I can."
This perplexed me. He didn't have a job, so what could he be doing to make it so difficult for him to have lunch? It turns out that between his church, his woodworking friends, his running companions, and the charity where he served. Moreover, he was really busy with his other errands. "I don't know how I ever had time for a job," he once told me.
So that's the first category.

The second group consists of those who like to stay at home, go for walks, vacation, watch TV, and use their computers or cellphones. These retirees do not make daily plans and prefer to be spontaneous in their day-to-day activities.

The third kind retires and wanders around aimlessly for a few months to a year. After that, they go out and start a second job. They NEED to work and feel like they're contributing to society. They don't have the hobbies or activities they need to retire and be content at home. For this type, being retired isn't enough.

We all agree that appropriate planning is required before retirement, regardless of the three categories we are. Unfortunately, most people make the error of planning for retirement a year or two ahead of time. This should not be the case. If you want to retire early for those still working, you will need to devote a significant amount of time to arrange your retirement in terms of money and non-financial matters. Keeping all of this in mind, you must enjoy your life while it is still possible! Carefully plan your retirement.

Also, before you quit your job, make sure your finances are in order. I've encountered people who put everything into saving for retirement just to have their health fail. And they ended up spending their money on medical treatment. All of their fantastic travel and entertainment plans were thrown out the window... so don't make assumptions... Before you retire, live your life...

What to do if your paycheck stops coming in

The main worry folks have as they approach retirement is whether they have enough money to retire. Of course, you shouldn't be fretting now you have this jackpot within your reach. However, it is only proper to address the topic since this book aims to "Help People Achieve a Great Retirement."
Eight methods to ensure you have enough money to retire and stay retired are outlined below.
But, before we begin, I'd like to make one clarification. I am not a financial advisor, and none of this advice should be followed without conducting a thorough analysis of your specific situation.
With that said, below are the 8 Steps to Make Sure You Have Enough Money to Retire and stay retired:

Put on Your Game Face

First, understand that retirement is the most important financial choice you'll ever make. Take it seriously and commit to putting in the time and effort necessary to make an informed decision. You'll need to put in some effort to get it perfect. Don't wing it, and don't be hesitant to employ a pro if you're unsure about completing the tasks on your own. It's a significant change to go from years of building your portfolio to drawing on those resources in retirement.

Create the Retirement Lifestyle You Want

It's crucial to keep in mind that you're attempting to figure out if you'll be able to retire comfortably. Before you can answer that question. You'll need to figure out how much your retirement will cost. A major chunk of the type of retirement you want to construct for yourself will be determined by that expense. Before crunching figures, make sure you have a good idea of what you want to achieve. Take some time to consider how you want to spend your retirement. How much money are you willing to spend on a vacation? Will you be downsizing? Will you spend more time entertaining yourself now that you have more spare time? Spend a few weeks dreaming and talking with your spouse. Make a list of your top priorities and keep them in mind while proceeding through the next few steps. The amount of time one spends thinking about retirement and the success of their transition into that retirement is essential. Consider this a financial investment in your retirement goals. It's coming, and the time you spend thinking about it before it happens will be well spent.

Keep tabs on your current spending.

Do you recall the first step? This is where you need to put on your game face. Sure, no one enjoys keeping track of their spending, but it's a necessary step in evaluating whether or not you'll be able to retire comfortably. Many people have no idea how much money they spend in a year, but it's impossible to tell when you'll be able to retire without an accurate estimate of your spending. In addition, you'll be better positioned to predict how your spending will alter once you retire once you've created a reasonable baseline for your current spending.

Plan Your Retirement Expenses

"Retirement is indeed a mathematical equation". You must remove as many "x's" as possible from the equation to finish the formula. Your retirement spending is one of the biggest unknowns, but that doesn't mean you should neglect it. In fact, the answer to whether you have enough money to retire is primarily determined by how much money you intend to spend in retirement.
Start by going over each spending category and estimate how it will change depending on the retirement you designed in Step #2, using the information you gathered in step #3.

Here are a few things to consider as you work through this:

- First, don't forget about health insurance. It's an essential cost item that could be a significant expense (particularly if you retire before Medicare becomes available).

- Plan for the future with caution (on the high side of spending). It's preferable to have pleasant surprises than unpleasant ones.

- Don't forget about taxes, especially if you plan to conduct Roth Conversions before being subjected to Required Minimum Distributions.

- Finally, creating a model that displays your expenditures throughout your retirement is beneficial. Your spending patterns will shift over time (for example, as you become older, you'll travel less but spend more on health care), As a result, keeping track of your retirement expenditures over time is critical to ensuring you have enough money in retirement and stay retired.

Determine Your Net Worth

Understanding your net worth is an integral part of retirement planning. You must first determine how much money you have to fund your retirement before assessing if you have enough money to retire. The Net Worth statement lists everything you own (your assets) and everything you owe (your Debts). Determine your net worth by subtracting your debts from your existing assets.

Calculate a Safe Withdrawal Rate

How much of your assets can you securely spend each year now that you know your Net Worth from Step #5? The Safe Withdrawal Rate is an important part of your retirement planning since it helps you figure out how much you can spend securely. For example, "a retiree should anticipate withdrawing 3 to 4% of their retirement funds annually."
Where you fit in that range is determined by various factors (risk tolerance, age, and asset allocation, to name a few), but as a general rule of thumb, think of 4% as a more aggressive strategy and 3% as a more conservative one. To make things simple, I consider both ends of the range to be "guardrails" for my annual spending range.

It's simple to add a few lines to compute your initial Safe Withdrawal Rate once you've completed your Net Worth. In this situation, you deduct assets that you're unwilling to spend in retirement (e.g., automobiles, home equity, though you might include some if you want to downsize). Simply deduct "Non-

Spendable Assets" to get "Spendable Retirement Assets," which you multiply by 3%, 3.5 per cent, and 4% to get the annual spending your net worth can support.

Calculate Your Retirement Income

Now that you know how much income you can expect from your investments, it's time to factor in the other sources of income to evaluate how your retirement income stacks up against your expenses. Again, make sure your figures are as exact as possible because this is the ultimate test of whether or not you have enough money to retire.

According to reports, 50% of workers do not have a reliable estimate of their future Social Security benefits. Make sure you're not one of them. Simply go to SSA.gov and enter your personal information. SS is an essential part of your retirement income that you don't have to guess about. First, you must determine when you will apply for benefits. However, the SSA website will provide you with information on several claiming ages. Next, add the proper Social Security amount into your retirement income benefit. Finally, include it in the multi-year cash flow estimate for the year you plan to start your benefits if you retire before you're eligible.

Continue the process for all additional estimated sources of retirement income after you've completed your Social Security estimations. Make a modest estimate if you're planning on working part-time in retirement to avoid a nasty surprise. Include any annuities or other income streams you expect and a pension if you're fortunate enough to have one. Finally, add a line for the Safe Withdrawal Rate, also calculated in Step #6.

Set up an Annual Financial Review.

Finally, keep in mind that your retirement will (ideally) last for many years. Therefore, you should conduct an annual evaluation to ensure you're on track as you progress through your retirement years. Having a yearly routine might help you stay on track with your safe withdrawal rate and avoid spending more than you can afford. It will most likely take less than two hours to complete this task.

☐

CHAPTER 2

When is the right time to retire?

This is a tricky one to answer because it is dependent on your own requirements and circumstances, as well as your plans for what you will do instead. We've all had days when we've felt like handing our boss a resignation letter and retiring to the good life. Though quitting your job early may sound like a dream come true, it can be a costly error if you aren't financially prepared to live without a paycheck. The following are some of the advantages and disadvantages of quitting your job at different ages.

Early Retirement: Before Age 65

Let's face it: quitting your work at this age has its advantages. Some workers are burned out when they reach their 50s and early 60s, so departing before the usual retirement age of 65 might be refreshing. The average retirement age for men is 64.6 years, while the average retirement age for women is 62.3 years. It's your chance to recuperate, whether it's through travel, new hobbies, or simply finding part-time work with less stress.

There is, however, a huge caveat here. Only a small percentage of people have the financial means to afford a long retirement. It's not always the case that the age at which you can retire and collect Social Security benefits is the same as the age you should retire. Even though you are eligible for Social Security at the age of 62, you will not receive your full monthly benefit until a few years later. It doesn't happen until the age of 66 for people born between 1943 and 1954. Anyone born after that has their age increased in two-month increments. For example, in 1955, the full retirement age (FRA) was 66 plus two months, and anyone born in 1960 or later has their age increased to 67.

If you apply for benefits at the age of 62, you will only receive 75% of the entire amount, which compensates for the fact that you will be receiving checks for a longer length of time. The benefit for your spouse is also reduced. They'll only get 35% of your total retirement income, compared to 50% if you wait until you're at least 66.

You'll most certainly need a sizable nest egg to supplement your Social Security benefits, especially if you retire early. Keep in mind that you won't be eligible for Medicare until you're 65, so if you have to get health insurance, you'll almost likely face high out-of-pocket payments.

Normal Retirement: Ages 66 to 70

For many people, the golden age of retirement is in their upper 60s—you're old enough to have amassed a sizable financial reserve while still being young enough to enjoy your work-free years. You'll receive your full Social Security payment at age 66 to 67 can make a significant impact, especially if you're in good health and plan to retire for an average or more extended period.

If you wait, you'll have a few more years to build up your tax-advantaged investment accounts. Investors over the age of 50 can make a catch-up contribution to their 401(k) or IRA annually. A regular IRA or Roth IRA can be funded with $7,000 if you are 50 years old or older. In addition, after you reach age 50, you can defer up to $26,000 of your salary in 2021 ($27,000 in 2022) if you utilize a 401(k) to save for retirement.
Waiting until you're 65 also means you'll be eligible for Medicare, which is often less expensive than individual insurance plans for seniors.

Late Retirement: Age 70 and Older

The benefits of working into your 70s are apparent if you enjoy what you do for a living. But, unfortunately, a long career may seem like the last thing we'd ever need for the rest of us.

However, think about the benefits. For starters, you'll have more time to put money aside. You'll also get the most out of your Social Security benefits. For example, if you were born between 1943 and 1954, your benefits would increase on a prorated basis until you reach the age of 70, when they are 132 percent of your total amount. Your benefit would grow by 124 percent if you were born in 1960.

As a result, if you plan carefully, you'll have more money to spend on the things you genuinely enjoy, and you'll be less concerned about outliving your assets. And if you stay healthy, you'll be able to enjoy the pleasure of retirement for many more years.

Most people look forward to the day when they can finally retire from their jobs. Even yet, constantly worrying about money isn't the best way to enjoy your golden years. That is why you should think about when you should retire rather than focusing on the age at which you are entitled to claim retirement benefits. Make sure you have the resources to make the most of this next stage of your life before deciding.

Marilyn S. Hiland

Why A Financial Advisor?

Many people gladly and openly seek the services of legal professionals, medical professionals, tax professionals, and even domestic professionals. Still, they rarely seek the advice of financial professionals when it comes to financial planning. Perhaps it's a legacy of our grandparents' generation and a fundamental lack of trust in sharing our financial condition with others. After all, it's money; we should be able to manage it, know where it's going, and what it'll do when it arrives, right? "Not precisely," I'm afraid I'd have to respond.

The rules and procedures for setting aside funds for the specific goal of financial retirement planning have grown just as complicated as the tax codes in our nation, which require a magic decoder ring to sort through and actually pay your taxes. One of the reasons they're so complicated is that many of them have particular and distinct tax benefits, either before or after the money is paid. Put another way, don't put those magic decoder rings away too quickly. In a few years, you might need them.

The bottom line is that a skilled financial planner can assist you in navigating the perilous terrain of taxes as it relates to your financial planning and much more. In addition, a qualified financial planner can most significantly alert you to opportunities you may not be aware of or may not be mindful of well enough. Their business is to be aware of the numerous chances to save and generate income for you and your family.

They can assist you with much more than retirement planning. They can help you plan for your retirement, your children's education funds, emergency money for life's minor mishaps, and a little extra to put toward those special purchases you could make along the way.

They can perform all of the above by examining your existing condition, future needs, current resources, and future objectives. They'll talk about any spending concerns that are bothering you, offer solutions, and assist you in developing a realistic plan for achieving your goals. However, their task does not end there. They'll keep track of your progress and, if required, make adjustments to help you get back on track with your budgeting.

Many people believe that they can do this on their own, and the truth is that some of them are. The vast majority of us, on the other hand, lack the discipline, willpower, and understanding of investment methods required to get a return on our assets comparable to that of a professional financial planner. Always keep the bottom line in mind when planning your financial retirement and your family's future. A qualified financial planner is well worth the fee if he can help you accumulate $100,000 or more in retirement assets.

One of the best benefits of working with a financial advisor is that you won't have to pay the hefty cost of learning from your mistakes. Instead of putting your money at risk, you can place their knowledge and experience to work for you. They can also assist you with estate planning and tax advice, so you don't have to fend for yourself. They can also assist you in determining your insurance requirements to safeguard those you leave behind. A good financial planner can help you maximize your retirement funds in various ways; the most challenging aspect for you as a customer is deciding to make the call.

Diversity Is Key in Retirement Planning

When it comes to financial retirement planning, diversification is the key to making a significant return. But, of course, you don't want all of your eggs to be in one basket. As a result, having numerous fingers in several pies at any given time, financially speaking, is a fantastic idea. But unfortunately, there are many different views of what it means to truly diversify your investment portfolio.

Some people assume that diversifying your portfolio is as simple as picking stocks from multiple industries rather than focusing on just one. When the Dot Com bubble burst, this was a major issue. During this historical period, many people acquired significant lessons and have taken them to heart. However, there is no guarantee that a major stock market meltdown will never happen again. If this happened, and your retirement goals, dreams, and assets were pinned on the stock market for survival, you'd be in deep, shark-infested financial waters.

I am not saying that a stock market crash is imminent or likely. In recent memory, the closest we've come to a stock market crash as a country was shortly after September 11th. The good news is that precautions were put in place years ago to avoid a disaster on the scale of "The Crash." This means that, while you may take a hit, the market will most likely recover if you are ready and able to wait it out. However, if you're putting yourself in a position where you'll have to rely only on equities, you should review your whole investment strategy and see where modifications may be made.

No financial choice should be taken without first consulting your financial advisor. My goal is to raise some questions and concepts that you might want to think about or, at the very least, discuss with your advisor.

My own preference is to have some money invested in mutual funds and some money invested in real estate, which can generate some type of monthly income. However, I'm not a gambler and have chosen a low-risk retirement planning and funding approach. When it comes to investing in their financial destiny, some people are significantly more daring than me. There are securities as an investment that provides a highly speculative ride for those willing to take risks. Securities are extremely risky for investors; inexperienced investors and some seasoned investors tend to avoid this type of investment. If you decide to invest in securities, I strongly advise you not to put your entire portfolio at risk.

Mutual funds are a safer bet when it comes to your financial future. There are no assurances here, but they are a safer option than securities. For many people, the difficulty with mutual funds is that there are so many to pick from that it is still a difficult decision for new investors to make. A good financial advisor can help you make these types of decisions while planning your financial future.

All-in-one funds are essentially mutual fund collections. These are a good alternative for people looking for a simple investment option that is relatively safe (though not extraordinarily conservative) to put their money in and watch. It slowly grows over time. All-in-one funds tend to become more conservative over time. This implies that as you become older, they'll be more conservative in how they invest your money to protect it while still growing it.

When it comes to safeguarding your gains, putting a modest percentage of your money in various areas will give you a far greater safety net. Consult your financial advisor about your intentions and any worries you may have. They're likely to be able to answer any questions or doubts you may have.

Marilyn S. Hiland

□

CHAPTER 3

Making financial plans for retirement

When planning for your retirement, keep in mind that your needs will be heavily influenced by how you live now and want to live once you retire. Many people live conservatively to save money for retirement and then live it up when they get there. The issue is that they're comparing their retirement lifestyle to their current one, which isn't a good comparison. In addition, most Americans earn barely enough money to make ends meet through their jobs. So for most Americans, finding any money to put aside for retirement is tricky at best and impossible in extreme cases.

When it comes to professional financial retirement planning, the first step is determining how much money you'll need to retain your current lifestyle after retirement and then proceeding from there. According to most estimations, you'll need to bring home 75% of your current take-home wage to maintain your current lifestyle. The assumption is that by not working, you will be able to remove numerous monthly expenses; however, some people discover that this is insufficient, so be careful when relying on this figure.

When planning your retirement, don't forget to account for inflation. Maintaining the same standard of living in the future requires more money. Remember that our expectations rise over time, and you must be able to live within your budget's restrictions when the time comes. Once you've reached retirement age, it'll be difficult to withdraw extra assets. As a result, it is in your best interests to plan ahead of time. The more simply you live today to save more money for your retirement, the better your chances of enjoying a better lifestyle.

You should also be wary of sacrificing the present to pursue a better retirement. In addition to meeting the requirements of today, you must be able to take holidays and save money for the things you want and need. Of course, we can't be certain that we'll be alive in retirement, but that's no excuse not to invest and save for that day. However, we should never forsake the present moment or our children's childhood for the sake of later retirement. As long as you're making considerable progress, you're ahead of a vast portion of the population, and you'll be able to invest larger sums of money in your retirement later.

Most people don't start thinking about their retirement plans until it's too late to make any significant progress. To secure the best potential outcome, start drafting financial retirement plans as soon as possible. Pay off large debts such as college loans, home loans, medical bills, car notes, and credit cards whenever possible. You no longer require these ongoing financial drains once you've limited or 'fixed' your income. You can start your investing account by having your bank automatically draft a portion of your check each pay period and your 401(k) or IRA contributions. You can also 'pay yourself a bonus by depositing additional funds if you receive other earnings, such as a bonus check at work or payment for services rendered outside of work. Make the most of every chance to increase your retirement savings.

Plans for Retirement

We all know that there is an increasing need in this country for us to take control of our retirement finances if we want to have any quality of life in retirement. If you don't know where to start regarding financial retirement planning or investment. There are a variety of programs accessible to us, and contributions to most of them are tax-deductible.

Setting up a set amount of money each month is, without a doubt, the most crucial aspect of retirement planning. However, until you invest that money, you will not be able to achieve your goal. One motivation to invest is to take advantage of compounding, which occurs when gains build on top of previous gains. For example, if you invest $100 one year and it rises to $110 the next, your gains the following year will be on top of the $110, not the initial $100. Compound growth can enhance rewards over time. Your investments will compound year after year, regardless of whatever account you choose. However, depending on the account, the amount you can save and the amount of tax you may have to pay in the future varies.

You can utilize the following accounts to save for retirement:

Individual retirement account (IRA)

Some individuals may associate the term IRA with the Irish Republican Army; however, an IRA is a tax-deferred investment account that allows you to save for retirement. Traditional, Roth, SEP, and SIMPLE IRAs are the four most common varieties of IRAs.

The last two are employee-generated, but individuals who fulfil the income requirements can open a Roth IRA. Individual accounts can be opened with the help of a broker.

Traditional IRAs

Individuals can contribute pre-tax dollars to a retirement investment account, which can grow tax-deferred until withdrawals are made (at age 59.5) or later. Traditional IRAs are held by custodians, such as commercial banks and retail brokers, who invest the funds in various investment vehicles based on the account holder's instructions and offerings. Traditional IRA contributions are generally tax-deductible. So, for example, if someone contributes $6,000 to an IRA, they can claim that amount as a deduction on their tax return, and the Internal Revenue Service (IRS) will not tax the earnings. However, when that person withdraws money from the account during retirement, the withdrawals are taxed at the individual's regular income tax rate. Depending on one's age, the IRS limits the amount that can be contributed to a traditional IRA each year. For the tax years 2021 and 2022, the contribution maximum for savers under 50 is $6,000. A catch-up contribution provision applies to people aged 50 and up, allowing for an additional $1,000 (for $7,000) in annual contributions.

Age limits on contributions to a traditional IRA were removed as part of the SECURE Act, which was passed at the end of 2019, so long the account holder has earned money.

Roth IRAs

Roth IRA contributions are not tax-deductible, but eligible withdrawals are tax-free, unlike regular IRA contributions. This means you contribute after-tax dollars to a Roth IRA, but you don't pay taxes on investment returns as the account grows. In addition, you can withdraw your contributions at any moment without penalty because you paid taxes on them. However, you cannot take earnings until you reach the age of 59.5, or you may be subject to a 10% early-withdrawal penalty.

When you retire, you can take money out of the account without paying income taxes on it. RMDs are not required for Roth IRAs. You don't have to take the money out of your account if you don't need it, and you don't have to worry about penalties if you don't. If you don't need the money, you can leave it to your heirs.

For 2021 and 2022, Roth IRA contributions are the same as regular IRA contributions: $6,000 unless you are 50 or older and qualify for the catch-up contribution, which increases the cap to $7,000.Contributing to a Roth IRA, however, is not available to everyone. In addition, contributions are phased off when your MAGI rises; thus, there are income restrictions.

SEP-IRAs and SIMPLE IRAs

Individuals cannot open SIMPLE IRAs or SEP-IRAs because they are benefits instituted by an employer, but self-employed or sole proprietors can.
These IRAs are comparable to traditional IRAs in terms of functionality, but they offer larger contribution limits and may allow company matching.

A simplified employee pension (SEP, or SEP-IRA) is a retirement plan that can be established by either an employer or a self-employed individual. Payments to the SEP plan are tax-deductible for the employer, and the company makes discretionary contributions to each qualifying employee's SEP-IRA. In essence, a SEP-IRA is a traditional IRA with the capacity to accept employer contributions. However, one of the most significant advantages to employees is those employer contributions are immediately vested.

A SIMPLE IRA is a retirement savings plan that most small firms with fewer than 100 employees can adopt. "SIMPLE" is an acronym for "Savings

Incentive Match Plan for Employees." Employers can make a 2% contribution to all employees' retirement accounts or an extra matching contribution of up to 3%.

Employees can contribute a maximum of $13,500 per year in 2021 ($14,000 in 2022); the limit is adjusted for inflation regularly. In addition, savers over the age of 50 can make a $3,000 catch-up payment, boosting their annual maximum contribution to $16,500 in 2021 and $17,000 in 2022.

Traditional IRA vs. Roth IRA vs. SEP IRA

These three retirement accounts have significant distinctions. First, you contribute tax-free money to a traditional IRA, which lowers your tax burden the year you contribute. However, when you withdraw money in retirement, they are taxed as regular income, and you must begin taking distributions at the age of 72. This makes it ideal for those who intend to retire in a lower tax bracket.

A Roth IRA works in the opposite direction. Withdrawals in retirement are tax-free since the money you put in has already been taxed. A Roth IRA is beneficial to people who expect to be in a higher tax bracket in retirement. Furthermore, because there are no required minimum distributions from a Roth IRA, you can leave the money in the account and pass it on to your heirs if you don't need it.

A SEP IRA is, of course, only available to self-employed individuals. It accepts employer contributions, which traditional and Roth IRAs do not, and all contributions are tax-free, meaning that payouts will be taxed as ordinary income in retirement. A SEP IRA's maximum contribution limit is significantly larger than a traditional or Roth IRA. In addition, employers can deduct their contributions from their taxes. Thus if a self-employed person is both an employer and an employee, they can deduct their payment. SEP IRAs were established to support small businesses in offering their employees and owners employer-sponsored retirement plans.

401(K) plans

A 401(k) plan is a tax-advantaged retirement savings plan offered by many American companies. It is termed after a section of the Internal Revenue Code of the United States.

When an employee joins a 401(k), they agree to have a portion of each paycheck automatically deposited into an investment account. The employer may match a bit or all of the contribution. The employee can choose from several investment options. The majority of them are mutual funds. In recent decades, employers have shifted the responsibility and risk of retirement savings to their employees, resulting in the rise of 401(k) plans and decreasing traditional pensions.

Employees must also select specific investments for their 401(k) accounts from a list provided by their company. These options usually include a mix of stock and bond mutual funds and target-date funds, which are meant to decrease the risk of investment losses as the employee nears retirement. In addition, guaranteed investment contracts (GICs) issued by insurance firms and the employer's shares may be included.

Traditional 401(k)

Employee contributions to a traditional 401(k) are taken from gross income, which means the money comes from the employee's paycheck before income taxes are subtracted. As a result, the entire amount of contributions for the year is deducted from the employee's taxable income, allowing for a tax deduction. The money contributed or earned is tax-free until the employee withdraws it, usually in retirement.

Traditional 401(k) account holders must take required minimum distributions (RMDs) after reaching a certain age. For example, owners of 401(k) plans who retire after the age of 72 are obligated to withdraw at least a specific amount from their accounts, according to IRS tables, based on their life expectancy. (The RMD was 70½ years old before 2020.)

Roth 401(k)

Contributions to a Roth 401(k) are withdrawn from the employee's compensation after deducting taxes. As a result, no tax deduction is available in the contribution year. When the money is withdrawn upon retirement, no additional taxes are due on the employee's contribution or the investment earnings.

On the other hand, Roth accounts are not offered at all employers. If the Roth is available, the employee can choose one or the other, or a combination of the two, up to the annual contribution limits for tax-deductible contributions.

Solo 401(K)

For self-employed business owners, a solo 401(k) is a tax-advantaged retirement account. It's similar to a major corporation's 401(k) plan, except it's only for the business owner and his spouse. You may be allowed to make pre-tax or after-tax (Roth) contributions and take out 401(k) account loans, just like with an employer's 401(k). However, your investment options and charges may differ depending on the account provider.

This plan is ideal for business owners who desire the greatest flexibility in their retirement savings. Although the solo 401(K) allows you to contribute more, it requires more paperwork to get started. As a result, you might wish to think about a SEP IRA or a SIMPLE IRA.

Traditional 401(k) vs Roth 401(k)

When 401(k) plans became available in 1978, employers and workers only had one option: the typical 401(k) plan. Then, in 2006, Roth 401(k)s were available. Former United States Senator William Roth of Delaware was a significant supporter of the Roth IRA legislation passed in 1997.

While Roth 401(k)s took a while to gain popularity, they are now readily available. As a result, employees are frequently required to select between Roth and traditional retirement plans.

Employees who expect to be in a lower marginal tax bracket after retirement should generally choose a regular 401(k) to take advantage of the immediate tax savings.

Employees who anticipate being in a higher tax bracket after retirement, on the other hand, may choose the Roth to avoid paying taxes on their money afterwards. There is no tax on withdrawals, which means that all the money deposited grows tax-free over decades. This is especially crucial if the Roth has years to grow.

In practice, a Roth 401(k) plan lowers your immediate spending power more than a traditional 401(k). This is especially critical if you're on a tight budget. However, because no one knows what tax rates will be in the future, neither 401(k) style is guaranteed. As a result, financial experts encourage clients to diversify their investments by putting a portion of their money into each.

Health Savings Account (HSA)

Like the previous tax-advantaged savings accounts, a Health Savings Account (HSA) is designed for consumers who have high-deductible health insurance policies (HDHPs). The employee or employer makes regular contributions to the account, which can be used to pay for eligible medical expenses not covered by HDHPs. For example, this annual payment can pay for medical, dental, eye services, and prescription medications.

HSAs are available to most people who have high-deductible medical insurance policies. Usually, the two are coupled together. As of 2021, an individual can contribute $3,600 to an HSA, and a family can contribute $7,200. In addition, individuals who are 55 years old or older before the end of the tax year are eligible for a $1,000 catch-up contribution. For persons under 55, the HSA contribution limits will increase to $3,650 for an individual account and $7,300 for a family account in 2022.

The annual contribution restrictions apply to both the employer and the employee's total contributions. An HSA can be opened at some financial institutions by qualified people who buy their insurance. Those with employer-sponsored health insurance make contributions to their HSAs through payroll deductions.

Any other individual, such as a family member, can contribute to an eligible individual's HSA. In addition, if you meet the eligibility conditions, you can contribute to an HSA as a self-employed or unemployed person. As of the first month after enrolling in Medicare, individuals cannot contribute to an HSA. They can, however, get tax-free payments for eligible medical expenses.

Important Points to Consider

HDHPs feature higher yearly deductibles than traditional health plans but lower premiums. In other words, the monthly payments are reduced, but the people covered are accountable for their medical expenses up to a specific limit.

The financial value of an HDHP's low-premium and high-deductible structure is dependent on your circumstances.
For the 2021 tax year, the minimum deductible required to open an HSA is $1,400 for a person and $2,800 for a family, and it will remain the same in 2022.

A yearly out-of-pocket maximum must also be included in the plan, which limits your out-of-pocket medical spending. For the 2021 tax year, the most are $7,000 for self-only coverage and $14,000 for families. The maximums for self-only coverage in 2022 are $7,050 for individuals and $14,100 for families.

Additional qualifying medical expenses are split between the individual and the plan when an individual pays qualified medical expenses equivalent to the plan's deductible level. For example, according to the contract, the insurer covers a percentage of approved expenses (typically 80 percent to 90 percent), while the plan bearer is responsible for the remaining 10% to 20% or a predetermined co-pay.

A person with a $1,500 annual deductible and a $3,500 medical claim, for example, uses this approach to pay the first $1,500 to cover the annual deductible. After that, the insured pays 10% to 20% of the remaining $2,000, with the remainder covered by the insurance company.

The plan typically pays extra medical expenses once the annual deductible is achieved in a given plan year, except for any uncovered costs under the contract, such as co-pays. To pay these out-of-pocket expenses, an insured can take money from an HSA.

Overall, HSAs are one of the most effective tax-advantaged savings and investment options available under the United States tax code. Contributions are tax-free, the money can be invested and grow tax-free, and withdrawals are tax-free as long as they are used for qualified medical expenses. As a result, they are often referred to as triple tax-advantage.

Medical costs tend to rise as a person gets older. So if you qualify, starting an HSA at a young age and allowing it to grow over time can go a long way toward protecting your financial future.

Marilyn S. Hiland

CHAPTER 4

Housing, Medicare, and Social Security

Housing Issues: An Overview

One thing that all retirees have in common is the need to reside somewhere. The issue is that if housing expenditures are not closely handled, they can become a substantial burden. According to recent data, retirees and soon-to-be retirees between the ages of 54 and 74 spend 32.8 percent of their monthly income on housing-related expenses, while those over 75 pay 36.7 percent. This is a significant portion of a set budget! Mortgage payments, property taxes, and repairs or improvements are examples of these costs. Occasionally, a change in their living arrangement is required.

One of the most challenging obstacles to overcome when a client considers a change in living circumstances is the psychological attachment to the home. Due to this problem, many people stay in their long-term primary residence for longer than financial sense would recommend. This is especially true if they have lived in the same place for a long time, are widowed, or have raised children there.

When considering living in a long-term primary residence in retirement, many aspects must be regarded as (later-stage retirement in particular). One consideration is the structure's suitability for retirement life. Are the restrooms equipped to meet the needs of an elderly retiree? Are there any stairs in the house that go to virtual spaces such as bedrooms, kitchens, living rooms, bathrooms, and laundry? Another consideration is purely financial. The home may be free of debt, but can the retiree keep it up? Property taxes, electricity costs, and exterior maintenance will all be incurred (like lawn care and snow removal). Roof maintenance, furnace or air conditioner repairs, or appliance failure are all possibilities.

Murphy's Law generally hits a surviving spouse with numerous of these circumstances within a short time after the first spouse passes away.

The state of the neighborhood is another factor that could influence a housing decision. In terms of physical condition and moral fabric, communities can decline with time. It's possible that what was once a reasonably safe neighborhood is no longer so.

Financial necessity may be the final straw. The ability of a retiree to use the equity in their home for living expenses may be critical to their economic well-being. Selling the house outright is one way to tap into this equity pool. In the following section, you'll learn more about these alternatives.

From an income tax standpoint, homeowners can sell their primary residence and deduct $250,000 of the gain from capital gains tax if they lived there for two out of the previous five years. For married couples filing a combined tax return can deduct up to $500,000 in gain. This substantial tax benefit may persuade consumers to view buying a primary property as a wise investment. This isn't always the case, but that's a topic for another day.

Options for Retirement Housing and Relocation Issues

Financial advisors are frequently called upon to help their clients with many aspects of their financial lives, including deciding whether to stay in their long-term residence or downsize. A life care community is a series of structures that start with apartment living and end with skilled nursing care if the retiree's needs develop that far. When retirees choose to live in a life care community, they will make a single payment to the facility's management firm. They will then pay a monthly cost that is usually the same regardless of their service quality. If the retiree proceeds to greater levels of care, the facility operator will rely on the initial lump-sum payment. The lump payment may be refunded to the retiree's heirs or the retiree themselves. Suppose the retiree leaves the institution due to death or a decision before using the lump money to pay for higher levels of care.

Unfortunately, those attempting to separate the naive from their money must always be on the lookout. This is especially common among the elderly. On the off probability that fraud is lurking in the background, it is critical to evaluate the financial health of the life care community operator before handing over the initial lump money.

Age-restricted housing is another option for a retiree looking to downsize. A big apartment complex or a series of patio homes with a central community structure offers services such as hairdressers, supermarkets, craft rooms, swimming pools, exercise centers, libraries, cooking lessons, or even access to a private golf course could be considered age-restricted housing. Part of the charm is that it's almost like returning to a college dorm, where many other retirees their age may be engaged in similar activities. This sense of belonging is enough to excite some people's attention. There are two types of age-restricted housing communities available. All residents in one scenario must be at least 62 years old. In the other option, the age limit is set at 55. In the second scenario, 80% of the residents must be over 55 years old. If a taxpayer has children who may need to return home after college or another life event, these age-restricted neighborhoods could be concerned. Due to the community's age limits, they may not be permitted to return home. Housing in age-restricted communities is also often smaller.

Some clients will wish to move to another state to be closer to family or live in a climate that suits their tastes or needs when they retire. Because this decision is difficult to reverse, it must be carefully studied. There are certain moving costs to consider, but there is much more to consider. For retirees, some states have quite varied taxation structures (income taxes, property tax rebates). The difference in inheritance taxation is a significant tax difference that is often overlooked. The client should also think about the available support mechanisms, such as access to medical facilities.

Innovative Housing Choices

Staying in the same house is a logical option to moving and downsizing. This option may necessitate some structural modifications, but it may be the best option in the long run. Could stair guardrails and/or automatic lifts be installed? Is it possible to change the flooring to make the house easier to maintain and have fewer tripping hazards? Is it possible to have the laundry, bedroom, bathroom, and eating area on the same floor? Is it possible to engage a service to maintain the grass and remove snow in the winter? If these issues are resolved, and the neighborhood is not an issue, staying in a long-term primary residence may be the best option. This allows the retiree to avoid dealing with the emotional ramifications of selling a home that holds so many memories.

If the retiree is having financial difficulties, a few innovative alternatives will allow them to stay at home while still tapping into their equity. A sale-leaseback arrangement is the first innovative solution. In this type of deal, retirees sell their home to someone else but sign a contract to rent it from them for a set period, usually a lifetime (along with as the retiree is alive or physically able or both). They are gaining access to all of the equity in the house, staying in it longer, and moving maintenance responsibilities to the new owner in this manner.

A reverse mortgage is another product of creative finance. This is a non-recourse loan. Thus any other assets owned by the retiree are secure from this creditor. The homeowners will get paid as long as they live in their homes. Payments could be made in three ways: a flat sum based on the borrower's age, a credit line that can be used as needed, or a set monthly cash advance. In essence, a loan balance will grow in the opposite direction of how the homeowner initially paid for his home. To employ this option, a homeowner must be at least 62 years old, and older retirees are allowed to borrow much higher percentages of the home's appraised worth due to their lower life expectancy. You may be asking what happens to the leftover home equity if there is any when the retiree passes away or decides to relocate. The extra equity in a reverse mortgage belongs to the retirees or their heirs, whichever is relevant.

Medicare Options

Medicare has a reputation for being difficult to understand. It has been divided into four sections to provide structure: Part A for hospital coverage, Part B for doctor's bills, Part C for managed care options, and Part D for prescription drug benefits.

Part A of Medicare covers inpatient hospitalization for qualified retirees. A retiree must fall into one of three categories to be eligible for Part A coverage:

- Someone who is at least 65 years old and is either eligible for or has chosen to defer Social Security benefits.
- Someone who is at least 65 years old and has opted out of Social Security during their working career.
- Someone who is not eligible for Social Security benefits on their own but is at least 65 years old and married to a fully insured spouse who is at least 62 years old.

Those at least 65 years old but who do not fit these criteria can enroll in Medicare by paying a monthly fee.

The retiree will have full access to benefits after their eligibility has been established. Benefit periods, or the length of time an illness necessitates hospitalization, describe Medicare Part A benefits. Each benefit period can last up to 90 days, and each benefit period must be separated by at least 60 days. Every Medicare beneficiary is given 60 lifetime reserve days, best explained with an example. Assume that a Medicare Part A-eligible taxpayer (Alexis) becomes unwell and needs to be admitted to the hospital. Because the sickness lasts fewer than 90 days, Medicare covers the entire hospital stay. After 61 days, Alexis becomes ill again. A new benefit period has begun, and Medicare will cover the following 90 days. However, he might have had a problem if Alexis had only stayed in the hospital for 20 days before taking a 45-day break before returning for another 90-day stay.

These two incidents are considered the same benefit period because the gap was less than 60 days, and 110 days of hospitalization surpassed the 90-day limits. This means Alexis would have to cover the cost of his hospitalization for 20 days. This might be a colossal cost! However, Medicare provides him with 60 lifetime days that he can utilize to deliver care at no cost to Medicare. Alexis might choose to have these 20 days deducted from his 60 lifetime days, which would pay the entire stay. After the 60 lifetime days have been used, Alexis is responsible for any extended stays. There is no limit to the number of benefit periods a person can have in their lifetime; however, the number of days in a benefit period and the number of days between benefit periods are limited.

Part B of Medicare covers lab tests, doctor visits, and outpatient surgeon expenses. Unless the patient requires admission to the hospital, an emergency department visit is considered an outpatient hospital service. It will also cover certain medically necessary supplies for recovery and treatment, such as a wheelchair. Part B usually does not cover prescription medications given in an outpatient environment. Part D is required for this. Some forms of therapy are also addressed. Part B is available for those who qualify for Part A coverage, but it requires the receiver to pay a premium. The monthly premium begins at $104.90 and increases with the retiree's income (adjusted gross income [AGI]). The premium is withdrawn from your Social Security income every month. Cosmetic surgery, dental treatment, vision coverage, hearing aids, and orthopedic shoes are services specifically excluded from Medicare Part B. (sometimes used for diabetics).

Part C of Medicare is a managed care alternative program, sometimes known as a Medicare Advantage plan. A Part C participant will pay a private insurance provider a Part B premium plus possibly a little more, and the Part C plan will replace Parts A, B, and D. The federal government will pay a fee to the insurance firm. Beneficiaries will be covered by the private insurance company rather than Medicare. For a limited service area, Medicare Advantage plans often give expanded coverage. This could be an excellent alternative for a retiree who does not anticipate doing much traveling. Medicare Advantage programs differ from Medigap policies, which are additional insurance policies that can be obtained to fill in the gaps left by Parts A and B.

Medicare Part D provides coverage for prescription drugs. Retirees must first enroll in Part B to be eligible for Part D, after which they can choose from a range of Part D plans. Payment of an insurance premium is required for each Part D plan. All types of Part D must include at least a base (standard benefit) plan, which starts with a $320 maximum out-of-pocket deductible and a 25% copay up to a total prescription cost of $2,960. After this point, Medicare will pay nothing until out-of-pocket expenditures surpass $4,700. At that point, the beneficiary will be enrolled in catastrophic coverage, which means they will pay the greater of a 5% copay or $2.65 for a generic drug or $6.60 for a brand-name drug. The donut hole refers to the coverage gap between $2,960 and $4,700. The Patient Protection and Affordable Care Act of 2010 aimed to close the donut hole by requiring those who fell into it to receive a 50% discount on brand-name pharmaceuticals and a 7% discount on generic drugs until the donut hole is closed.

Social Security's retirement program

The Social Security Administration (SSA) does more than just issue retirees monthly benefits. It's a group of government programs that provide benefits to retired or disabled workers and their dependant or surviving family members. Although this chapter focuses on retirement benefits, let's take the time to review all four programs. After all, you may one day meet the requirements for more than one—for example, you may be eligible for benefits based on your own and your retired spouse's retirement. Check the Social Security Administration's website for eligibility, although in general, you can only receive one of these benefits, not both. The four programs that make up Social Security are:

Benefits for people with disabilities. If you're under 65 and meet the job requirements, you may be eligible for disability benefits under the Social Security program's medical rules. These benefits will be nearly equivalent to what you would receive if you retired.
Benefits for dependents. You and your minor or disabled children may be eligible for payments based on your spouse's earnings record if you're married to a retired or disabled worker who qualifies for Social Security retirement or disability benefits. Whether or not you rely on your spouse for financial support is

true. Married beneficiaries should consider if a combination of one Social Security benefit and one dependent benefit or two Social Security retirement benefits would provide them with a larger payment (assuming both partners are entitled to one). Retirement or dependent benefits may be awarded to each individual, but not both.

Benefits for survivors. You qualified for disability or Social Security retirement benefits. You and your minor or disabled children may be eligible for payments based on your deceased spouse's earnings record if you are the surviving spouse of a worker.

Retirement benefits. This program pays workers benefits based on how long they've worked and how much they've paid into the system, regardless of their financial need. If you've worked in Social Security-covered occupations for at least ten years, you should be eligible for retirement benefits. The SSA regularly sends out a document called "Your Social Security Statement" because forecasting this is an essential first step in budgeting for retirement. If you haven't gotten this estimate of how much money you'll receive each month once you retire, contact your local Social Security office or request a copy at www.ssa.gov/mystatement. If you prefer not to provide information via the internet, you can print and mail the Social Security Statement Request Form (SSA-7004). Alternatively, you can calculate

THE BASIC RETEIRMENT PLANNING GUIDE FOR 50+

your benefits by going to
www.ssa.gov/retire2/calculators.

CHAPTER 5

How to Invest and Where to Invest

What Investment Options Do You Have?

With inflation eating away at your retirement funds, you'll need to take steps to protect and expand your retirement income. Here's a rundown of some common investments and their expected returns and hazards. We'll go through them in greater depth later in this chapter.

Cash: *Lowest Risk, Low Returns*

Cash accounts, such as savings accounts, money market accounts (MMAs), and certificates of deposit (CDs), offer a lower rate of return than stocks, bonds, mutual funds, and other financial instruments. However, you gain security in exchange for any losses in profits, dividends, or interest income. The risks are minimal when your money is in a cash account because these accounts are typically insured by the FDIC (see "How the FDIC backs you up," below). The Federal Deposit Insurance Corporation (FDIC) insures only bank money market accounts; money market mutual funds are not. Even so, you shouldn't place the majority of your retirement savings in cash accounts. Interest rates are also low (typically under 4%) and are sometimes even lower than the inflation rate.

Bonds: *Low to Moderate Returns with Low to Moderate Risk*

Why are the risks associated with bonds lower than those associated with stocks? Because: (1) interest rates are typically fixed and unaffected by stock market fluctuations; (2) The institutions issuing these loans are stable entities such as cities, governments, and large enterprises, except for lower-rated so-called "junk bonds." Government bonds, such as US Treasury bonds (with $1,000 minimum investments and minimum terms or "maturities" of ten years or more), because they are backed by the US government, they are viewed as the safest investments. Some municipal bonds are guaranteed and regarded as low-risk investments. Furthermore, interest income generated by most municipal bonds is tax-free on federal and state levels if you live in the state where the bond was issued. Of course, no matter how low the risk, any bond has the danger of default—that is, the government entity or firm may be unable to repay the debt. (It's worth noting that the US government has never missed a payment of principal or interest.) Treasury Inflation-Protected Securities are another option for conservative investors (TIPS). These are guaranteed to pay a fixed premium above the Consumer Price Index, modified annually.

What is the most efficient approach to buy bonds? Although bonds can be purchased directly, most people who enter the bond market do so through a bond fund, which is a mutual fund that invests primarily in bonds and other debt securities. These mutual funds come in a variety of shapes and sizes. To name a few, you may put your money into a government bond fund, a mortgage-backed bond fund, a global bond fund, a high-yield bond fund, or a municipal bond fund. The benefit of the fund is convenience: you can leave bond selection decisions to someone else (the fund manager). Bond funds provide a lower level of certainty than buying and holding a bond directly.

Individual Stocks: *High-risk, variable-return investments*

As you're undoubtedly aware, a share of stock is an ownership interest (or "equity interest") in a corporation. When you own stock, you make a profit when the value rises above its price, or if the corporation pays out a regular dividend, stockholders profit. There is no assurance that any stock will be returned.

Is it that risky to invest in the stock market?

The difficulty with buying individual equities is predicting which ones will explode (or implode) first. In that respect, speculating on the success of individual stocks is similar to speculating on cards in Texas Holdem. Sure, there's a degree of skill required. Like experienced market analysts, professional gamblers can evaluate trends and grasp statistical probability. Even if you're aware of economic trends, you'll need to determine which stocks will profit (or survive) from them. And if you're wrong, you could lose all of your money.

What is the best way to acquire stocks?

You shouldn't be buying individual stocks if you're asking this question. Many top stock analysts now work as fund managers for mutual funds. So, before pursuing a career in the stock market, consider whether you can outperform Fidelity or Vanguard's fund managers. If you answered no, you should skip buying individual stocks and go straight to our section on mutual fund investments. If you still want to try your luck in the stock market, here are some ideas:

• Invest a tiny amount of your savings in the stock of numerous different companies. You're unlikely to substantially jeopardize your retirement if you don't gamble with more than 10% of your money. Also, don't invest more than 3% of your retirement funds in a single company's shares. If you come out ahead in the short term, you can use your gains to make additional profitable investments in the future. Avoid investing in individual stocks if you have a credit card or other debt, as the high-interest rate would likely offset any profits you might make.

• Invest in things you're familiar with. Most stock market experts advise using personal and professional insights gained from your knowledge and experience in a particular area. If you have the time and willingness, read financial journals to learn more about firms and industries you're already familiar with, rather than about companies you're unfamiliar with. If you're considering investing in a particular sector, you'll almost always be better off buying a good mutual fund in that area.

• Expand your horizons. Investing all of your money in one, or even two, stocks are always risks, no matter how blue the chip. Instead, a mix of investments is always the best approach. If you think the industry will do well, consider buying shares in a few strong businesses to ensure you get the actual winner.

- Select stocks that you intend to own for a long time. If you buy and sell regularly, taxes and trading charges will reduce your return compared to a simple index mutual fund purchase.

- Stay away from day trading. When you buy and sell a stock or other investment in a single day, this is known as day trading. It's used by investors who try to profit from modest stock swings by never holding a stock past the closing of trade on the day they bought it. Day trading usually necessitates the acquisition of costly software. After all of the expenses are taken into account, the odds of making a profit are minimal.

Mutual Funds: *Diverse Risks, Diverse Returns*

A mutual fund collects money from several people and invests it in stocks, bonds, cash, or these asset classes. Funds generate income for investors by producing profits from fund assets (dividends or interest gained on cash assets or bonds) or by generating income (capital gains from stocks or bonds that the fund has sold or gone up in value). The fund managers are constantly purchasing and selling investments. You buy shares in a mutual fund to invest in it. The price of one share in a mutual fund fluctuates daily, just like the price of an individual stock, depending on the performance of the underlying investments.

Every mutual fund has management who makes investment decisions to achieve the fund's objectives. These objectives may differ by the fund—for example, some funds prioritize steady, long-term growth with low volatility, while others prioritize quick, short-term growth. You may find a mutual fund for almost any firm you want to invest in and at any risk level you want to take.

The following are some of the most essential advantages of mutual funds:

• Ease of usage: Investing in a fund, moving your money from one fund to another, or switching investment companies is simple—whether you do it online, by mail, or over the phone.

• Low-cost professional assistance. You get a professional managing your money for a fraction of the cost of a standard brokerage fund or financial adviser.

• Diversification is important. Funds diversify money across a variety of assets, lowering risk.

The disadvantages of funds are the same as those of any other investment.

- Risks and money march hand in hand. There's no guarantee that a mutual fund will make money, that your shares will appreciate, or that the fund will be impervious to market crises.

- Fees might cut into revenues. Even though fund fees are generally low, they can add up to a significant portion of your profits. Avoid mutual funds that take more than 1.5 percent of your assets each year as a fee (1.5 percent is the average). Look for "no-load" funds that don't charge you a commission upfront (which can eat up around 3 to 6 percent of your investment). It's simple to compare the fees of several funds on the internet.

Investing in and Profiting From Real Estate

Our investment talk would be incomplete if we didn't mention real estate investments, precisely rental properties and real estate investment trusts (REITs). After all, in recent years, real estate has appeared to be a safer choice than the stock market.

So, should you invest in real estate or the stock market?

If you want a hands-on investment that you can see and touch while still being time-consuming, local real estate investments should be considered, provided you are familiar with the market. Rental income and property value appreciation are two potential sources of revenue from real estate investments (with no capital gains taxes until the property is sold). As a result, real estate investments are a popular backup investment option for retirees. Keep your money in mutual funds or bonds to avoid the hassles of maintaining or improving a structure and dealing with tenants. Here is some additional information to assist you in making your decision.

In the field of real estate investing, your major options will be:

- **Commercial real estate**. Unless the property is tiny and you are very familiar with the area, it's typically better to avoid commercial real estate investments. Otherwise, the risks of investing in office buildings, malls, and industrial real estate—or creating partnerships to invest in these properties—usually outweigh the benefits.

- **Residential real estate.** Condos and single-family homes can be complicated investments. If you intend to rent the property, the rental income must exceed the mortgage payments, property taxes, and management costs—an increasingly difficult task given that mortgage payments alone in many parts of the United States exceed average rents. Multifamily properties are usually a better investment, though they are more expensive. One option is selling your home and renting one of the units in a multi-unit building.

- **Real estate investment trusts (REITs).** Suppose you think real estate prices will outperform other forms of investments. In that case, you can invest in a REIT, a trust that acts like a real estate mutual fund, gathering investors' money and investing it in commercial and sometimes residential real estate. In recent years, REITs have been high-flying investments.

Real estate investing' drawbacks

Lack of diversification. You probably already have a house, condo, or co-op apartment if you're like most people. As a result, you should consider placing more money into this investment. Purchasing stock and bond mutual funds may be safer to diversify.

- **Your lack of experience**. Because there is no daily market to assist you in identifying a fair price for local real estate, unlike stocks and bonds, casual investors sometimes rely on the advice of local real estate agents looking for a commission. The all-too-common result is that they pay too much for a home and then sell it for too little.

• **Time demands**. After a downpour, if water flows through a tenant's skylight, the owner is out with a ladder to fix it in the middle of the night (or by the following day at the latest). Put your money somewhere else if this doesn't sound like you. Hiring a property manager is an option, but it will cost you extra money.

• **Potential liability**. Real estate owners are seen as rich targets for renters, visitors, or even a trespasser who claims to be harmed. To secure your assets, you may need expensive insurance or the formation of a corporation or limited liability company.

• **Taxes due on the property**. You must pay property taxes each year that you own the property to reap the eventual benefit.

• **Dealing with other people**. Many people with additional cash organize a joint venture to buy the property with family members, friends, or coworkers. What happens if several other investors decide to bail out when the market is down? You'll almost certainly be compelled to sell at a loss or raise funds to buy out the others.

THE BASIC RETEIRMENT PLANNING GUIDE FOR 50+

CHAPTER 6

Staying Active in Retirement

People are living longer and longer these days, so there is so much emphasis on good aging. Today, retirees are looking for ways to retain a high quality of life for as long as possible to keep medical bills low and stay active in their retirement years. Longevity doesn't always imply an excellent quality of life, which is why it's critical to take charge of your health as you become older. Preventative interventions will become increasingly crucial as Baby Boomers reach retirement age and begin to encounter senior-related health difficulties.

Healthy aging can necessitate a total revamp of one's life, including exercise, nutrition, and lifestyle adjustments, for most people. While this may seem daunting, take heart: it's never too late to start living a healthy lifestyle. Retirees now have a multitude of chances to live their greatest lives ever as medical developments and scientific studies become more advanced. Even small moves in the right direction might serve as a foundation for bettering your health. It's easier than ever to live well into old age by combining a balanced diet, exercise, medical treatment, and other factors.

Given the lack of exercise and a poor diet, even younger people can have a poor health-related quality of life. As we become older, our bodies become less capable of dealing with the challenges that come with leading an unhealthy lifestyle, which leads to health problems. Non-physical changes occur as we age, such as the death of loved ones, declining talents, and retirement from employment. Emotional health is equally as essential as physical health, and retirees must ensure that their wellness plan integrates healthy practices across all requirements — physical, emotional, and mental – to live a healthy and balanced life.

Marilyn S. Hiland

EAT HEALTHY FOODS TO HELP YOU LIVE A HEALTHY LIFE.

You are what you eat, and it's critical to make sure you're putting the correct fuel into your body as you become older. However, some changes, such as a loss of taste, a slowed metabolism, and a diminished sense of smell, might occur during this time. All of these factors can lead to a lack of nutritional foods in our diets. You may also be unable to go grocery shopping or prepare meals, or you simply do not like to be bothered. I understand — you've earned a break. Eating healthy, however, does not have to be difficult. You may incorporate healthy behaviors into your diet in a variety of ways:

Speak with a family member or a health care practitioner about community initiatives that provide retirees with healthy food options.

If you're able to cook, make sure you're getting plenty of fruits, veggies, fiber, lean protein, whole grains, and healthy fats. This combination will make you feel full and energized while also allowing your digestive system to function as efficiently as possible. If you're on a low-sodium or low-sugar diet, experiment with different herbs and spices to add flavor to your meals.

Even if you're not thirsty, remember to stay hydrated. Water keeps you energized, lubricates your joints and muscles, and moisturizes your skin.

Make mealtimes a social meeting spot for friends and family. Gather your family, friends, and neighbors for a feast. This keeps you socially active and encourages you to eat regularly, even if your appetite is low.

You will feel better, maintain a healthy weight, and reduce your risk of acquiring illnesses such as diabetes, arthritis, and heart disease if you eat properly.

EXERCISE CAN HELP YOU REMAIN HEALTHY.

According to a new Swedish study, exercise is the most important factor in extending one's life. And the advantages can begin almost immediately. Even patients in their 70s who began exercising can enjoy significant benefits! Here are some of the ways that regular physical activity benefits seniors:

- Prevents memory loss and lowers the chances of dementia.

- Endorphins are a type of neurotransmitter that helps to improve mood and emotional well-being.
- Chronic pain is lessened.
- Muscle mass is increased, which enhances metabolism.
- Assists retirees in sleeping more deeply.
- Posture, balance, and flexibility are all improved.
- It strengthens your immune system.
- Maintains a healthy weight

Start slowly if you haven't exercised much (or at all). Even 10 minutes a day might make you feel better and improve your circulation. Add additional time to your workouts as time goes on, and experiment with different types of exercise. What is important is that you find something you enjoy doing.

However, exercise does not have to be confined to physical activities. It's just as important to keep your gray cells active and stimulated by exercising your mind. Puzzles and memory games are fun, but so are learning a new language, volunteering, taking up a new activity, or simply spending time with friends and family. Daily mental challenges keep your mind agile, lower your risk of cognitive decline, and keep you feeling young.

STAY HEALTHY BY KEEPING A POSITIVE ATTITUDE.

Let's face it: growing older is difficult. You can deal with this in one of two ways: by being pessimistic and dreading the future or by remaining optimistic and welcoming the change that lies ahead. You can minimize stress, enhance your mood, and give yourself an overall sense of well-being by embracing and letting go of the things you can't control and looking forward to the things you can.

You don't have to sit back and let life pass you by just because you're getting older. There are still many ways for you to live a purposeful life, and you still have much to offer the world. Being retired is a wonderful stage of life since you have more time to pursue the things you've always wanted to do, such as start a charity, write your memoirs, or start a new job.

What to Do in Retirement: 20 Big Ideas

You probably have more alternatives for how to spend your time in retirement than you ever did before. You also don't have to limit yourself to just one aim, activity, or pursuit. Perhaps you'll seek a career in painting. Or maybe skydiving is more your style. Do you think that's insane? I know a woman who took her first skydiving at the age of 79 and had a fantastic time! Is this something she'd like to do again? No. She didn't do it because she had other ambitions.

Retirees do not live a life of stagnation. Things change, and your interests may change as well. Retirement is a period when you get to create your own rules and adjust them as needed. What you desire today may be drastically different from what you want in a few years when you retire. It's also time to start thinking bigger now that people are living longer than ever before.

Here are 20 strategies to establish a perfect retirement life balance that is both peaceful and thrilling, rewarding, straightforward, and challenging:

#1 Do what brings you joy.

Many of the entries on this list mention doing something extraordinary. However, that isn't the purpose. It is not necessary to be the best, first, oldest, or most.

It shouldn't matter if you're keeping up with the Jones' when you're retired. It's now or never to do what makes you happy. You have the option of appreciating the small things or swinging for the fences. You may make a difference in the lives of your loved ones or improve lives in your community by volunteering. You may be able to make a fortune doing what you love, or you may be able to make ends meet while following your dreams. It shouldn't matter how big or small your projects are.

Think long and hard about what you want to do after you retire.

#2 take a look around the world, or at least your little portion of it.

Travel is near the top of many retirees' bucket lists of things to do. Some retirees have always desired to visit a specific city. For others, a more steady travel schedule is far more appealing.

A memorable trip does not necessitate crossing an ocean. You may spend your entire life traveling across North America and never see anything. Even traveling within your state can provide you with opportunities you weren't aware of.

A traveller's life is diverse. Some people like to travel by RV, while others prefer to travel by rail. Flying, of course, will take you almost everywhere. Retirees can be resourceful when it comes to lodging If you wish to stay in a hotel, go ahead. Alternatively, consider Airbnb, a site that connects travellers with private B&B experiences in the United States and throughout the world.

Consider becoming an Airbnb host and renting out your property while you travel the world, allowing your home to pay for your travels.

#3 Attend summer camp

Summer camp isn't solely for children; it's just as enjoyable now as it was when you were a child. The adult version is less likely to give you poison ivy and more likely to provide a variety of experiences that far outweigh any wilderness camp your children may have attended. A camp for adults offers fishing, fitness, race car driving, acting, and other activities.

If you have a hobby, there is likely a camp for it. What about a spa retreat? A directory of adult camps can be found on SummerCampHub.

The options list is intriguing. Do you want to fight zombies? "Inspiring" new age encounters? Traditional camp activities combined with nighttime cocktails? There's a camp for everyone.

#4 seasonally relocate

Going south for the winter isn't a new idea, but what about going north when the heat gets too much? You may want to be closer to your children on occasion, but not all of the time. It's also a possibility if you've never spent your holidays in the mountains (or at the seaside).
Purchasing a vacation property somewhere else allows you to have the best of both worlds without sacrificing your roots. However, seasonal relocation isn't the only option.

Consider a housing swap:

If you live in the north and want to go south (or any other configuration), house swap services will match you with another homeowner who desires the opposite, and you will temporarily switch residence as featured in the film The Holiday, international house swappers exist. Try IntervacHomeExchange.com and HomeExchange.com.

Look into seasonal jobs:

Are you concerned about your financial situation? If you migrate seasonally, you'll almost certainly be able to find work serving holidaymakers! Consider working as a campground host, ski slope attendant, lifeguard, and so on... Coolworks.com is a good place to look for seasonal job openings and ideas.

#5 Plant a garden

Working outside while the weather is nice, at least for some individuals, makes life worthwhile. Gardening has also been shown to add years to your life, according to research.

Gardening can be done in different ways. Some individuals prefer the aesthetics of a flower garden to growing veggies. You could also do both, with plenty of options in any direction. There's a lot to learn about plant care. If it's your passion, you may graft new plants, become an experienced composter, or take care of roses and veggies to sell at a market.

#6 write a book

You don't need any formal education to create a book, and you can write whatever you want. A how-to book could be inspired by personal experiences. If you've had a fascinating life, you may have enough material for a riveting book.

You have two options if you plan on writing your book.

Amazon allows you to write, upload, make a book cover, and more if you wish to self-publish.
If you prefer traditional publication, the route will be a little more difficult, but you'll have a team on your side.

#7 What Should You Do When You Retire?

Become an instructor.

As a second profession, several brand new instructors enter the field. You'll almost certainly need more schooling if you wish to teach in a traditional setting, such as public or private schools or colleges. Find out more about certification, salary, and other topics. And, if you want to make a difference, the United States is the place to be. The Department of Education releases a list of teacher shortage locations across the country.

However, teaching in a traditional classroom is not the only option to make a living:

Create an online course:

Make money by teaching people all over the world by creating an online video course. You choose what to teach on Udemy, design the curriculum with their tools, and help students find you. Perhaps your family's cooking is the best on the planet, or perhaps you're an amazing knitter. You can be a teacher in whatever field you're an expert in.

Tutoring is an excellent method to supplement your income.

Another rapidly growing industry is tutoring, both in-person and online. Sign up for a site like Wyzant, which matches tutors with students in need of assistance.

#8 Renovate your home

Retirement is a good time for renovating if you plan to retire in your own house or even if you wish to sell. You can make changes to your home to match a new lifestyle or renovate it to increase its value and sell it for a higher price.
A new master bedroom on the first floor, a safer bathroom, kitchen renovations, a new hobby workshop, or whatever else your heart desires might be included in the improvements. This is also an excellent opportunity to make sure your house is in good working order. If you need a new roof or HVAC system, replacing it now will save you time and money in the future.

#9 Work as a consultant

Just because you're retired doesn't mean your abilities are worthless. Many employers are confronted with a dilemma. Employees who are fresh out of college are on the cutting edge in many ways.

However, seasoned professionals with a wealth of expertise will retire at some point. Because consulting allows you to work less and make more decisions, it may be a good fit for you.

#10 Keep your retirement strategy on track.

Regardless of what else you're doing on this list, we all need to keep our retirement plans in check.
Every 3-6 months, you should evaluate your financial situation. You need to know if you'll have enough money in retirement to do everything you want for the rest of your life (no matter how long that turns out to be).
These calculations can be made easier with the aid of a decent retirement calculator. The NewRetirement Planner is a comprehensive and highly customizable application that saves and updates your information. The planner also provides you with fast feedback on the impact of any changes on your overall financial health.

#11 One of the most important things to remember in retirement is to maintain your vitality.

Having somewhere to go. Having people (or animals) who look to you for help. Keeping to a schedule. Having a social life. Having a goal in mind. Always learning new stuff. All of these activities have been scientifically proven to help you stay healthy, happy, and vital.

#12 Learn to play an instrument: Anything is possible!

Even if you don't consider yourself musical, there's a good chance you'll find an instrument you enjoy playing. The piano and the guitar are both popular for beginners. Remember that your voice is an instrument as well. You could also take banjo and singing classes.

Learning to play an instrument is not only beneficial to your life, but it is also a never-ending endeavor. Even the world's greatest musicians continue to practice and master new skills.

Learning new things is also a terrific strategy to maintain your brain in good shape.

#13 Get in the best shape of your life

As the saying goes, health is wealth. Another lifelong passion is fitness, which can improve retirement life in practically every aspect. You'll have more energy, a healthier body, and a more positive attitude as a result.

Fitness has so much diversity that you will never get sick of it. Yoga, Pilates, spinning, and other classes are available. Weight training also helps to treat arthritis, enhance balance, promote bone density, control weight and diabetes, strengthen the heart, and improve sleep quality.

#14 Increase the number of people in your circle of friends.

Too often, as time passes, retirees become more and more attached to their homes. What was once a large circle of friends may begin to decrease until only a handful remains in your life. While there's nothing wrong with spending time alone, having friends keeps you connected to the rest of the world and gives you a sense of purpose.
Finding some younger pals is also a wonderful idea. Spending time with someone who is older or younger than you open your eyes to new experiences and vice versa.

#15 Attend your high school reunion, whether it's your 35th, 40th, or any other.

There's nothing like a high school or college reunion to get you thinking about your accomplishments and plans.
As we consider retirement, we need to take stock of our life and develop new goals.
A reunion can be a great chance to reconnect with old friends and perhaps be reminded of our passions, which can help us plan how we want to spend our retirement years.

#16 become an expert in any field.

You've probably experienced many life events and fantasized about others that never materialized. Have you ever fantasized about being a fantastic chef but lacked time to pursue your dream? Or have you ever considered improving your mechanic abilities but never got around to it? Retirement is the ideal opportunity to transform a hobby into something you can master. You may perfect your woodworking talents or develop the next big thing in pottery. Develop a strong desire to become an expert in your chosen field. Then pass on what you've learned.

#17 consider the future.

Because of their longer lives, most retirees have a lengthier retirement than their forefathers or mothers. However, just because you live to be 100 does not guarantee you will feel the same at 98 as you did at 70. Everyone eventually loses some of their desire to go-go-go.

Re-evaluate your retirement plan regularly and make any necessary revisions. The more you plan ahead of time, the less likely you are to find yourself in a scenario where you want medical attention but cannot afford it. Wish to be closer to family but can't move or any of the numerous unforeseen events that may arise over time.

#18 become a financial expert.

While you're saving and investing actively in preparation for retirement, you may want to seek the advice of a professional. However, there will come a moment when you must switch to maintenance mode. If you continue to learn and stay up with what's going on in the financial world, you should be able to handle it on your own after that. It is possible to create one's financial expertise. Reading all you can, even good blogs, is a good idea. Also, start watching finance-related TV series. You'll soon understand what disintermediation, econometrics, and other terms imply without needing to consult a financial planner because you'll be the expert.

#19 keep up with the times.

The millennial generation is the first to have grown up in a world where the internet has always been, in some form or another. Older generations lived without it or any of the other modern conveniences. And, at times, technology can be baffling.
Keeping up with technology in retirement gives you a lot of freedom and allows you to take advantage of more of the advantages of living in a quickly changing world. So don't be frightened. Accept technology and continue to study.

#20 Spend quality time with your grandchildren

If you're looking for ways to pass the time in retirement, consider activities you may do with your grandchildren. Being a grandfather or grandmother is a truly unique experience. You get all of the magic of the child with none of the burden.
Spending time with your grandchildren during retirement can be a lovely experience. You can talk about topics that matter to you and learn about things that matter to them. They can help you stay young while also allowing you to help them mature.

CHAPTER 7

CONCLUSION

Some of us are in professions that are our life's calling, and going to work is as much fun as it works for us. You enjoy what you do, and the prospect of not doing it every day feels more like a punishment than a prize towards the end of life. Changing your lifestyle due to retirement appears to be as much a surrender as it is a long vacation. And you're not the type to accept that retirement is unavoidable. It may come after you, but it will have a tough time doing so.

Retirement may not be for you if you are that type of person because retirement isn't for everyone. And why should you be forced to fulfill someone else's fantasy just because some individuals have the idea of quitting their jobs just as things were getting better as a means to enjoy their last few decades? If you enjoy what you do, waking up and going to work is just as important as eating well and getting enough rest to keep your blood flowing and your metabolism running smoothly. People are born with an insatiable urge to work. It's what defines us, and it's what motivates us to give to society and be compensated for our efforts. As a result, you should not feel bad if you are a retiree who is still doing what you love.

Not stepping down, but stepping into the role of senior adviser, chief counsel, and the wise old owl of the office is one approach to increase your role in the career you love. For the young puppies coming up, your decades of experience are a treasure trove of insight and a source of teaching. This is one of the reasons why many organizations around the country are recognizing the value of maintaining senior citizen employees rather than pushing them to retire.

This is a significant departure from the mindset that the old had to make way for the new for far too long. The elderly are now a valuable resource for teaching the young how to properly do things. Business is discovering what many cultures have long known: elderly persons are a treasure to be valued and cared for, not discarded.

www.ingramcontent.com/pod-product-compliance
Lightning Source LLC
Chambersburg PA
CBHW070111230526
45472CB00004B/1214